"The next time you start to reach for your referee's whistle, reach for *Help! The Kids Are at It Again: Using Kids' Quarrels to Teach People Skills* by Elizabeth Crary. Her approach takes parents beyond the usual adage that 'They're only after your attention.' . . . This book is full of examples that could have been taken from any home in America with more than one child."

—*The Boston Globe*

1997 Winner of the Family Channel Seal of Quality Award

The Family Channel Seal of Quality is your assurance of positive family entertainment

HELP!

The Kids Are at It Again

Using kids' quarrels to teach "people" skills

ELIZABETH CRARY

Illustrated by Mits Katayama

Parenting Press, Inc.
Seattle, Washington

Printed in the United States of America

ISBN 1-884734-08-1 paperback
ISBN 1-884734-09-X library edition

Library of Congress Cataloguing-in-Publication Data
Crary, Elizabeth, 1942–
Help! The kids are at it again : using kids' quarrels to teach "people" skills / by Elizabeth Crary.
p. cm.
Includes index.
ISBN 1-884734-09-X (library). -- ISBN 1-884734-08-1 (pbk.)
1. Child rearing. 2. Sibling rivalry. 3. Interpersonal conflict in children. 4. Social skills in children. I. Title.
HQ769.C925 1997
649'.1--dc20 96-32502
CIP

Parenting Press, Inc.
P.O. Box 75267
Seattle, Washington 98125

Contents

Words of encouragement

Rebecca enjoyed her first child, Anna, and was delighted to be having another. She believed that her children would be playmates for each other. She would give them lots of attention and love, and they would never fight.

When Heather, her second child, came home from the hospital, all was well until Heather began to move around. Then conflict began. Anna would not let Heather touch anything. As Heather grew, Anna began to boss her around.

Rebecca was distressed by all the quarreling and wondered where she went wrong.

Over the past several years I have had many parents in classes share experiences similar to the one above. They have asked for ideas to "deal with sibling rivalry and quarrels." I noticed that many of the behaviors parents were concerned about with siblings were the same behaviors children exhibited with their friends.

That observation led me to look at sibling conflicts in the light of skills children need to get along together. It appeared that sibling jealousy did not completely account for the fights. In this book I have identified four "people" skills kids need to get along with siblings and others. For example, Anna's behavior may be due to a need to set boundaries on "her things" and to learn about power. She may not feel jealous at all.

Sometimes people wonder why children in some families appear to get along great all the time. There are several possible reasons. First, some children have very easy temperaments and do not get into hassles with siblings or others. Second, some siblings learn the skills they need easily without struggling with their siblings. Third, some children live in such unhealthy households that the only way they can survive is to bond solidly together. These children never quarrel, and they put their siblings' needs above their own.

The good news is that parents can teach their children the skills they need to be more socially adept. Rebecca, above, can teach her children to set and respect boundaries, and to use power respectfully. When you teach these skills, quarrels will not stop entirely, but children will have the skills to work out their differences. These skills will be useful with siblings and friends now and with other people later on in life.

Why can't the kids get along?

Danny, age $2\frac{1}{2}$, poked baby Nathan in the stomach. When Nathan began to cry, Mom rushed over. She pulled Danny away from the baby, and said, "Stop that. You know not to hurt him. Hurting's bad. Go to your room for a time-out."

When Danny didn't go, Mom took Danny's hand and led him to his room. On the way, Danny cried, "I sorry. No time-out. Please, Mommy."

The more frequently Mom gave Danny a time-out, the more it seemed Danny bothered his brother.

Maria, age 2, wanted the toy Rosa, age $3\frac{1}{2}$, had. When Rosa put it down for a moment, Maria grabbed it. Rosa screeched, "Give it to me." Maria ignored her, and a battle over the toy began again.

"I want to go, too! Why can't I go?" Anthony wailed as he watched his older brother James pack for a camping trip. "I know," Anthony announced, "Dad can take me."

James explained again, "You can't go camping unless you are a member of the troop. And Dad is one of the scout leaders, so he has to go."

When James left to find his boots, Anthony took James's flashlight and hid it. When James couldn't find the flashlight, he told his mother that Anthony had taken it.

Devonne, age 10, was tired of reading. She was tired of drawing, beading, watching TV, and doing homework. She didn't want to clean her room or help her mom.

She watched Eddie, her four-year-old brother, build a tall tower. She picked up her book and headed for the door. As she passed her brother, the book slipped from her hand and demolished his tower.

Eddie screamed, "You broke my tower!"

Devonne replied smugly, "It was an accident."

Calvin, age 9, was sitting on the sofa watching a video. Erica, age 4, came over and started poking his feet. He told her to quit it. She giggled and continued. He tucked his feet under him to protect them. Then Erica tried to push him over. She lost her balance, slipped off the sofa, and hurt her head.

What's going on with the siblings?

Many people believe all conflicts between children result from jealousy or sibling rivalry. Although that may be true in some situations, conflicts are more likely due to developmental issues. Siblings are often the most convenient people to work on these issues with. When the tasks are learned, conflicts decrease.

How much sibling conflicts decrease will be affected by how conflicts in general are handled in their family, and by how parents nurture the new developmental skills children learn.

Siblings need specific skills to get along together. They need constructive ways to:

- Feel like they belong
- Establish personal boundaries
- Deal with their feelings, and
- Solve problems

Each of the situations above represents a skill the child needs to learn to get along in healthy ways:

- Feel included in the family (Danny)
- Negotiate (Maria)
- Deal with feelings (disappointment or anger) (Anthony)
- Deal with boredom (Devonne)
- Notice and respect personal boundaries (Erica)

We will revisit each of these situations as we look at how to help siblings learn the basic "people" skills.

Children learn people skills at different rates. Some children seem to be born knowing how to get along well. Others learn by trial and error on their own. Some need help to learn.

Four necessary people skills

There are four basic skills that children need to get along with their siblings and with other people.

Achieving belonging. Children need to feel they are a part of a group. The need to belong is a basic human need. Children will do whatever they must to be recognized. They will even break rules and anger their parents if they have to in order to get attention. Sometimes siblings want a parent's attention. Other times, they want a sibling's attention. This same need drives older children to join gangs when their need for belonging is not met.

Setting & respecting boundaries. When children are born, they start to separate from their mothers. They learn what is them and what is not. As they explore the world they learn that there are boundaries. They can have some things and not others. They can go some places and not others.

Dealing with feelings. Children need to understand their feelings and develop constructive ways to cope with them. They need to learn that other people have feelings, too. Siblings present many opportunities to learn about feelings.

Solving problems. Children need skills to get what they want constructively. They need to learn to trade, wait, bargain, and negotiate. They need to know that there are different kinds of power and that power can be used constructively or destructively.

In a perfect world children would learn these skills as naturally as they learn to walk and talk. However, most children need to be taught people skills.

The easiest time to teach people skills is during the corresponding developmental stage. However, the skills can be learned at any time. As we go through this book we will refer back to the children and their conflicts introduced on pages 9 and 10.

Some children complete one stage before moving on to

the next. Other children take unfinished business into the next stage. When that happens you can have a four-year-old working on power issues and still trying to deal with his feelings, for example.

Developmental stages and tasks

Age	Stage	Developmental task
0–6 mo.	Being	To grow and trust
6–18 mo.	Explore	To explore their world
18–36 mo.	Think & feel	To distinguish between thoughts and feelings To express feelings constructively
3–6 yrs.	Power & identity	To observe how people use power To decide how to be powerful To decide what men and women do
6–12 yrs.	Structure & peers	To develop a structure for living in the outside world

Developmental issues in sibling conflicts

Siblings provide each other with many opportunities to work on developmental issues. In the chart on page 14 you can see how different siblings can learn different skills at the same time.

Clearly, every situation has learning opportunities for both children. How smoothly things go will depend, in part, on the siblings' temperaments.

Developmental tasks and skills

Task: To feel loved and connected

Baby cries and takes up lots of parent's time. Older sibling feels ignored.	Younger sibling needs to learn to comfort herself and trust that help is coming.	Older sibling needs to learn constructive ways to gain parent's attention.

Task: To explore the world

Mobile baby starts to tear older sibling's book. Sibling gets upset.	Younger sibling needs to learn she may not explore everything she can see.	Older sibling needs to protect possessions (boundaries) by keeping things out of reach.

Task: To learn to deal with feelings of self and others

Toddler has a tantrum when she can't have her sister's new doll.	Younger sibling needs to learn how to handle her feelings (anger, frustration, boredom).	Older sibling needs to learn to deal with angry sibling and other angry people constructively.

Task: To decide how to be powerful and get needs met

Preschooler wants something his sibling is using and grabs it.	Younger sibling needs to learn several respectful ways to get what he wants (trade, wait, negotiate).	Older sibling needs to protect possessions (boundaries) by establishing clear rules and consequences, and getting help when needed.

Task: To develop a structure for living in the world

Child has a bad day at school, then picks on her brother at home.	Younger sibling needs to learn to identify personal distress and deal with it directly.	Older sibling needs to learn to evaluate the accuracy of sibling's statements, and to get support when needed.

Temperament

Each person, child and adult, has his or her own temperament. It is made up of nine personality traits, and is usually constant over time.

A person can be intense on one trait and mellow on another. Most people fall between the extremes. As you look at the temperament traits in the chart on page 16, mark where each of your children falls on the scale.

Each trait is valuable in some situations and a handicap in others. The traits that are frustrating in children, like persistence and high energy, are valuable in adults. The challenge for parents is to channel those traits in constructive directions. For more information about temperament, see *Know Your Child* by Chess and Thomas in "Other interesting books" (page 89).

Temperament affects sibling conflicts

Temperament traits dramatically affect how the developmental tasks are played out with siblings. An intense child will be louder when he is upset with a sibling than a child with a quiet temperament. A physically active child is more likely to hit or shove than a physically quiet one. The following examples show you how temperament can affect situations between children.

Maria takes Rosa's toy. If Rosa is a quiet, adaptable, distractible child, she will soon find something else to play with.

If both Maria and Rosa are intense, persistent, and inflexible, they may struggle for a long time over the toy.

Tomi wants to play chase with his big brother Joji. If Joji has low energy, is irritable, persistent, and wishes to read his book they may be quarreling soon.

If Joji is cheerful, energetic, and adaptable they will probably be chasing each other around soon.

Nine temperament traits

Activity level

High activity and energy levels	Low energy and rarely fidgety

Intensity

Intense whether they are happy or mad	Quiet and reserved most of the time

Approach/withdrawal

Automatically approach new people or situations	Initially resist most new things

Adaptability

Adapt quickly to change regardless of their initial opinion	Take weeks or months to adapt

Sensitivity to physical world

Extremely aware of light, sound, temperature, and texture of clothes, etc.	Totally unaware of the physical world

Persistence

Stay with a task for a long time, even for things they have difficulty with	Move from one activity to another frequently

Regularity

Have a precise internal clock. Eat, sleep, and toilet at the same time each day	Have an irregular clock. May sleep six hours one night and 12 the next

Mood

Born happy, cheerful, and optimistic	Often irritable and upset

Distractibility

Easily distracted by activities going on around them	Unaware of or rarely distracted by people, noise, or activity

Conflicts between two children with strong temperaments will be more noticeable than conflicts between children with milder temperaments. Although it is difficult to change temperament, you can give children skills to cope with their differences. The next chapter offers tools to deal with conflicts.

STAR parenting

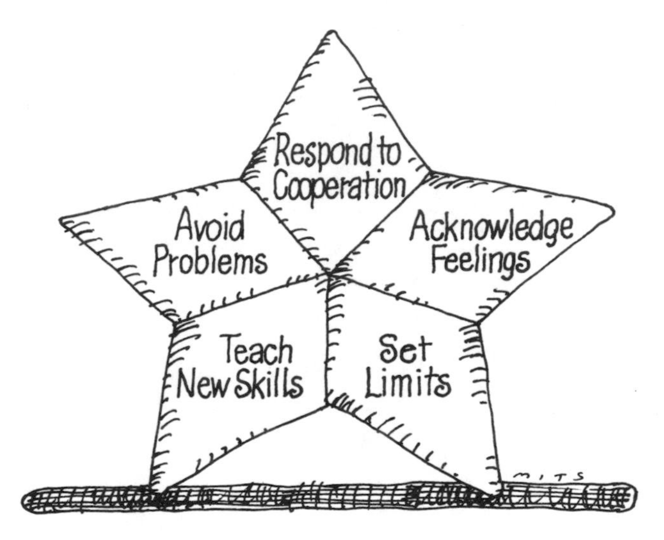

Figuring out what skills siblings need is one thing. Learning how to teach your child skills is another. In this chapter we will look at one way to deal with sibling behavior—STAR parenting. STAR parenting offers a *process* for solving problems and *fifteen tools* to use. The tools are organized in five areas or points. You can use this information to deal with your children's behavior and to teach them new skills.

STAR process

The STAR parenting process is based on the word *star.* Each letter stands for a different step:

- S - Stop & focus
- T - Think of ideas
- A - Act effectively
- R - Review & revise

Stop & focus. Acknowledge your feelings. For example, "I'm really frustrated with all the bickering."

Calm yourself, if you are upset. Take a deep breath or look outside. You can find more ideas on dealing with feelings on pages 44–53. Ask yourself, "Is this behavior really important? Will it make a difference five years from now?"

Look at your children's behavior. How frequent is it? How long has it been going on? Consider your long-term goals for these children. Can their behavior be used as a springboard for teaching your values?

Think of ideas. There are many possibilities for dealing with behavior in each situation. The more different ideas you consider, the more likely you are to find one that will work. You can use STAR tools or get ideas from:

- Talking to friends and relatives
- Reading books
- Listening to a lecture
- Going to parenting classes

Act effectively. When you have several different ideas, decide which one you will try first. Consider your children's needs, your needs, and what you want your children to learn. Plan your approach. Get help or support if you need it. Then *do it!* The best plan won't work if you don't act.

Decide how long you will try one approach before revising your plan. There is no magic amount of time to wait. When you change how you respond to a behavior, a situation will sometimes get worse before it gets better. Children may try harder to get the response they expect, before they try a new behavior. However, there is no point continuing an approach that is not working after a reasonable try.

Review & revise. Very few plans work completely the first time. Most plans need to be revised. It usually takes three to five attempts to find something effective. Sometimes ten or more revisions are needed. Hang in there until you find something that works.

STAR points and tools

Effective parents use five points: avoid problems, teach needed skills, acknowledge feelings, notice desired behavior, and set reasonable limits. The five points are equally important.

Avoid problems. Reduce the number of conflicts so you can work on what is important.

Tools	*Examples*
Reduce stress	Allow enough time.
Change things	Store a preschooler's toys where a toddler can't reach them.
Two yeses	"If you want to be left alone, you can draw on the table or in your room with the door closed."

Respond to cooperation. Increase good behavior by noticing it when it occurs.

Tools	*Examples*
Give attention	Spend time with your children while they are pleasant to each other.
Praise	"Thank you for letting your sister look at your new book."
Reward	"When you ask me for help instead of hitting, you may have a sticker."

Acknowledge feelings. Recognize children's feelings without judging or agreeing.

Tools	*Examples*
Simple listening	Just listen. No advice.
Active listening	"You're disappointed that you didn't get a new dress today, too."
Grant in fantasy	"Wouldn't it be fun to have a magic wand? Whenever you wanted something new, you could wave the wand and you'd get it."

Set reasonable limits. Establish boundaries and expect child to test them.

Tools	*Examples*
Clear rule	"Touch gently."
Consequences	"If you hurt someone, you play alone for a while."
A better way	"I have two kids who both want to use the wagon. What can we do so they can both be happy?"

Teach new skills. Offer skills needed for living within the family and out in the world.

Tools	*Examples*
Modeling	Treat the children the way you want them to treat each other.
Shaping	First day, show a preschooler how to put his toys out of the toddler's reach. Next day, help him put all toys up. Then, help him put some of the toys up. Finally, remind him to put the toys up.
Re-do it right	"Oops. You forgot to ask Molly for the truck. Let's go back and do it right."

You can read more about the STAR parenting process and tools in the book *Love & Limits: Guidance Tools for Creative Parenting* by Elizabeth Crary, page 90.

Using the STAR process to teach sibling skills

When you really want to change a behavior, use the STAR process. Stop and focus on the problem. Think about what you need, and what each of your children needs. Decide what skills they need to learn to get along together.

Act effectively by selecting an idea to start with, making a plan, and implementing it. After you have tried the plan for a while, review your success and revise the plan if necessary.

The next four chapters will show how STAR parenting can be used with four challenging situations:

- Wanting to belong
- Establishing boundaries
- Dealing with feelings
- Solving problems

Skill 1
Achieving belonging

Akio, age 4, was driving trucks. Suzo, age 9, was on the floor drawing a large picture. Every minute or so, Akio would zoom a truck over and it would bump Suzo. She would tell him to quit it and return to her drawing.

Eventually, he hit Suzo so hard she dropped her pen and it made a big black spot in the rainbow. She turned to yell, "You're a stupid little brat! Why don't you go get lost?"

Then Akio went downstairs and told his mother that Suzo called him names.

Danny poked baby Nathan in the stomach. When Nathan began to cry, Mom rushed over. She pulled Danny away from the baby, and said, "Stop that. You know not to hurt him. Hurting's bad. Go to your room for a time-out."

When Danny didn't go, Mom took Danny's hand and led him to his room. On the way, Danny cried, "I sorry. No time-out. Please, Mommy."

The more frequently Mom gave Danny a time-out, the more it seemed he bothered the baby.

What children need to know about belonging

One of the basic needs of human beings is to belong. Much adult and child behavior is designed to meet that need. For children, attention is a sign of belonging. Most children believe if they cannot get attention, they do not belong.

Children need to know that it is okay to want attention. They need to learn how to get attention in different ways and from different people.

Each child is welcome in this family. Children need to feel accepted and appreciated as family members. This is particularly true when a new baby arrives. The older sibling may feel excluded or unwanted. The child may think, "Why are they focusing so much attention on the baby? That must mean they don't want me anymore."

It is okay to ask for attention. Some children believe that it is not okay to ask for attention. So they set up situations where they will get attention without asking for it. Usually the quickest way to get attention is to hurt a sibling.

Children can get attention in different ways. They can ask for a hug or kiss directly. They can ask for help drawing a picture or building a fort. They can ask for company.

Children can get attention from different people. In addition to parents and siblings, there are grandparents, neighbors, and friends who can give attention. Some children get attention from store clerks and people on the street. Attention helps children feel like they belong.

Parent's role in children's learning

Children need attention whether it is convenient for grown-ups to give it or not. With some children the demand for attention feels unending. Strange as it seems, many children will prefer negative attention (a spanking) to being ignored.

Give children messages that affirm belonging. Messages like, "You are special to me," "I like to be with you," "I'm glad you are my son/daughter," or "I enjoy having you around" tell children they belong. Children need these messages all the time, and especially when their behavior is difficult.

Accept that your children need attention — no matter how inconvenient the timing is. With babies and very young children, you need to give the child attention quickly or arrange for someone else to. With older preschoolers and school-aged children you can sometimes negotiate a time to meet their needs.

Decide how you want your child to ask for attention. To a child attention is an indication of belonging. If children need your attention they will get it. The choice for parents is how they get that attention. Children can ask for a hug or hit a sibling. What they choose will depend on how the parents respond. You can choose ideas from the list on page 26, or make up your own ideas.

Give attention to appropriate behavior. For example, if you want your daughter to ask for a hug instead of pulling her sister's hair, you need to stop immediately to give her a hug when she asks for one.

Thirty ways to give attention

Quick loving
give a hug
sing "okay"
blow a kiss
sprinkle love dust
ruffle hair
stroke arm
smile

Quick help
pin back barrette
tie a shoe
sound out a word
shuffle cards
balance a block
watch child a moment
hold hands

Short activities
read a book
give child a bath
make a group hug
help child call a friend
kick the soccer ball
play "Go Fish"
play catch
make a snack

Involved activities
bake cookies
plant flowers
go to the park
make a doll dress
fix toys
paint teen bedroom
have a party
go fishing

Using the STAR parenting process: Belonging for Danny

Using the STAR parenting process from the previous chapter, Danny's mother could think through her children's problem in this way.

Stop & focus. Danny's mom, Stacy, might think, "Danny is barely 2½ years old. He used to have my complete attention; now he has very little. Whenever he pokes Nathan I come running. If Danny really wanted to hurt Nathan badly he could have, but he just made him cry a bit."

Think of ideas. Ideas that might help Stacy:

- *Avoid the poking* by not leaving the kids together.
- *Notice gentle behavior.* She might say, "I noticed you stroked Nathan's arm. He liked that. Did you see him smile at you?"
- *Decide how she wants him to ask for attention.* She could say, "Danny, when you need me, say 'hug' and I will stop what I am doing and give you a hug."
- *Offer two yeses.* For example, "Danny when you want attention you may ask for a hug or show me something."
- *Model asking for attention.* "Danny, may I have a big kiss?"
- *Reduce conflict by giving him regular attention each day.* For example, "When Nathan takes a nap we will have some special time. I will set the timer for 20 minutes and we can do whatever you want."
- *Acknowledge his frustration.* Stacy might say, "It's frustrating to share me with Nathan."
- *Acknowledge his feeling of being left out.* "I'll bet you feel left out sometimes when I nurse Nathan."
- *Clarify limits.* "Touch gently. It's okay to want to be with me, and you must touch Nathan gently."
- *Establish a different consequence.* "Touch gently. If you make Nathan cry, I will pick Nathan up and leave the room."

Act effectively. Stacy might think, "The time-outs are not working, so I'll try a different approach. I'll teach Danny how to ask for attention directly. I want him to ask for a hug. When he does ask I'll give him one immediately. And as I work on this I won't leave the two children together alone."

Review & revise. "I'll work on this for a week. If there is improvement I will continue. If not, I will pick Nathan up and leave Danny alone if he hurts Nathan."

Using the STAR parenting process: Companionship for Akio

Using the same STAR process Akio's mother could think through her challenges this way.

Stop & focus. Akio's mother, Tomiko, might recall that his annoying behavior has increased since his sister Suzo started back to school. When Suzo comes home she wants to be alone for a while and Akio wants to play.

Think of ideas. Tomiko might think of these options:

- *Avoid the conflict.* "I could play with Akio myself when Suzo comes home."
- *Reflect Akio's feelings.* "It's frustrating to wait all day for Suzo and then not be able to play with her when she comes home."
- *Teach Akio to offer choices.* Tomiko might say, "If you ask Suzo to play with you she will probably say, 'No.' But she might play if you offered her a choice. You can ask her if she would rather read to you or play super heroes."
- *Give Akio two yeses.* Say, "You can invite Paul over to play or you can call Grandma."
- *Reward Akio when he waits.* Say, "You asked Suzo if she would play with you. Here is a card with a star on it. When you get ten stars we can __________. "
- *Model asking to spend time together.* "Akio, I'd like to spend some time with you. Could we play ball together?"
- *Make a rule.* "Respect people's needs." In this case Akio could let Suzo alone for 15 minutes. Then Suzo could play with him for 15 minutes.
- *Teach Akio that there are several ways to meet his needs.* Sit down with a large piece of paper. List all the ways he can get attention: play with Suzo, call Grandma, play with Paul next door, help Mom.

Act effectively. Tomiko might think, "I want Akio to know his needs are important and so are Suzo's. I want him to ask to play and then respect Suzo's decision. I'll acknowledge his feelings, and reward him when he waits."

Review & revise. "If that doesn't work, I'll give him two yeses, or play with him myself."

Wise words

Caring for kids can be exhausting emotionally and physically. Take good care of yourself so you can take good care of your children.

Take care of your basic needs. Get enough sleep. Eat regular meals. It is hard to give attention to children when you are tired or hungry.

Get regular physical exercise. Exercise helps reduce feelings of anger and frustration. It also increases stamina. When one gets enough sleep and exercise it is easier to be patient.

- Put on a video and do aerobics with your kids.
- Go for a brisk walk when your partner gets home.
- Make arrangements to swap babysitting with a friend and go to an exercise class.

Arrange to take breaks. Everyone needs a little time to themselves. Do something that is enjoyable to you.

- Read a book
- Take a leisurely bath
- Work on a project
- Play a musical instrument
- Putter in the yard
- Cook something special

When children are young it is often hard to find time to take a break. The following are some ways to find time:

- Join a babysitting group.
- Hire a mother's helper to play with your kids while you are at home.
- Take a sack lunch to work and have fun by yourself.
- Ask a friend to babysit the kids while you relax.

In this chapter, we have looked at the task of belonging. All people need to feel that they belong. They get that feeling when they receive attention and recognition. A parent's task is to help children develop skills to get attention in constructive ways.

Skill 2
Exploring boundaries

Maria, 2½, wanted Rosa's doll. When Rosa, age 3½, put it down for a moment, Maria grabbed it. Rosa screeched, "Give it to me!" Maria ignored her, and a battle over the doll began again.

Devonne, age 10, was tired of reading. She was tired of drawing, beading, watching TV, and doing homework. She didn t want to clean her room or help her mom.

She watched Eddie, age 4½, build a tall tower. Then she picked up her book and headed for the door. As she passed Eddie, the book slipped from her hand and demolished his building.

Eddie screamed, "You broke my tower!"

Devonne replied smugly, "It was an accident."

Calvin, age 9, was sitting on the sofa watching a video. Erica, age 4, came over and started poking his feet. He told her to quit it. She giggled and continued. He tucked his feet under him to protect them. Then Erica tried to push him over. She lost her balance, slipped off the sofa, and hurt her head.

From the time a baby is born she is learning about boundaries. She no longer gets food automatically, she must ask for it. The hands that wave in her face are hers. She can control them. She is discovering what is her and what is not her.

This exploration eventually leads to creating boundaries. The abilities to create healthy boundaries and respect other people's boundaries are essential parts of acting responsibly.

What children need to know about boundaries

Children need to know what they have control over and what they do not. They need to know that there are different kinds of boundaries and that these change with time. They need to know that they are in charge of their boundaries. They need to learn strategies for dealing with boundaries.

Some things are mine, some things are not mine. From a child's perspective, things in the world fall into three groups.

Always mine. No one else uses them: pacifier, shoes, clothes, special toy or blanket.

Not mine. These things belong to someone else: Dad's shoes, Mommy's glasses, Dad's books, Mommy's purse, the telephone, Molly's doll, Paul's truck. One must ask to use them.

Partially mine. These things the child may use without asking. However, other people have access to them as well. For example, the child has partial ownership of the sofa, blocks, television, grandma, and parents.

Boundaries change. They change as a child grows. For example, when a child is born he believes that his parents are always "mine." Sharing them is not necessary. Then, when a second child is born, he discovers he must share his parents. This is often very hard.

Boundaries also vary with the person. Rosa might have been willing to let Grandma hold her doll, even though she did not want her sister Maria to play with it.

Children control their own boundaries. Children need to know that their boundaries are like a fence with a gate. They decide who may come in and who may not. For example, if someone wants to tickle them or take a toy, they can say either, "Yes" or "No."

People have several kinds of boundaries. When children are small they are primarily concerned with personal boundaries and with their possessions. As children get older, space, thoughts, and time boundaries also become issues.

Observing boundaries

Boundary	Disrespectful	Respectful
Personal (or body)	Giving reluctant child a hug.	Asking, "Can I give you a hug?"
Possessions	Putting Zack's old red boots on his little sister without asking.	Asking and respecting answer, "May Emily wear your old red boots?"

Observing boundaires (cont.)

Boundary	Disrespectful	Respectful
Body space	Reading the comics over child's shoulder.	Asking, "May I read the comics with you?"
Thoughts and feelings	Making fun of child's feelings. "Look at the cry baby."	Accepting the feelings without trying to change them. "That must really hurt."
Time	Telling a friend your daughter will be happy to babysit.	Saying, "I think Sarah is available to babysit. Call and ask her."

There is a difference between "telling" and "tattling." Children often run to the parent when a sibling bothers them. There is a delicate balance between getting help and getting someone else to do your work for you. *Telling Isn't Tattling,* by Kathryn Hammerseng (page 90), explains the difference this way:

> ***Tattling.*** Children tattle when they want to—
> - get attention,
> - make someone else look bad, or
> - ask for help before they have tried to solve the problem.
>
> ***Telling.*** Children tell when they—
> - want protection for themselves or other people,
> - want protection for property (theirs or others), or
> - feel scared or in danger.

Children need to be encouraged to try to solve their problems first and to get help when they can't.

Tools to maintain boundaries

Children can establish boundaries by stating them clearly, moving or creating barriers, problem solving with the other person, or getting help.

Clarify the boundaries. Give kids words to establish their boundaries. Here are some examples:

- "Don't poke me. It hurts."
- "I'm not done playing with . . ."
- "Don't look over my shoulder. I need more space. I'll give you the newspaper when I'm done."
- "Ask me before you say I'll do something. I may have plans."

Move herself or her things. If a child doesn't want someone to touch her, she can move. If she wants to draw without the toddler scribbling on her paper, she can work on a table. If she wants to play with Lego® blocks and the toddler wants to touch, she can build in the playpen or behind a safety gate.

Try to resolve the problem. If a child has clarified his needs and is ignored, it may help to find out what the other person wants. Children can do this by asking directly, or by guessing.

Direct question. For example, "I asked you to stop poking me and you are still doing it. What do you want?" The answer could be anything. The other child may want him to move over, or she may want to play with him. When he finds out, he can decide what to do next. If the other person will not tell him, he is no worse off.

Make a guess. A guess can be a real guess, or something outrageous. The purpose is to start a conversation. For example, "I asked you to stop poking me and you are still doing it. I guess you must want me to tickle you. On the count of three I will begin." If the other child wants attention, then gentle tickling might do. If she wants something else, she may say so. Again, the purpose is to start the problem-solving process.

Get help. If someone is hurting a child or her things and she can't get them to stop, she needs to get help. She can find help by getting someone or calling out for help. She can explain what the problem is, what she tried to do, and what she needs. Remember, no one deserves to be hurt.

For example, Emily might say, "When I was sitting on the sofa watching TV, Steven poked me. I asked him to stop, but he wouldn't. So I moved to the floor. He moved down there and started poking me again. I moved to the other side of the room and he came over and continued to poke me. I want to watch TV without being poked."

When you as a parent have ideas about what kids need to know about boundaries, you can help kids apply the skills to real situations.

Parent's role

Respect children's boundaries. Insist others respect boundaries, too. When a child is done cuddling, let her go. When she tells Granddad, "No kiss," suggest he blow her a kiss instead.

It is important to respect children's body space when you can. However, if the child is at the doctor's and doesn't want a shot, you can explain that health and safety issues come before personal preferences. Then offer some choices like, "Do you want to hold my hand or sit on my lap?"

Model setting clear boundaries. For example, if your toddler hits your face, say, "Touch gently" and turn him around so he can't hurt you. If he grabs your glasses, say, "Daddy's glasses" and stand up so he can't reach them. If your preschooler wants to play with your purse, put it in your room and close the door.

Make and enforce family rules about boundaries. Here are some rules you might want to consider:

- Stop when someone says, "Stop."
- Knock before you enter someone's room.
- Ask before you use something that belongs to someone else.
- You are responsible for what your body does—accident or not.
- Respect people's need for space.

Insist children respect other children's boundaries. In the beginning you will need to remind them and follow through with consequences if needed.

For example, if Eddie said, "Stop tickling" and Devonne continues, Dad could say, "Devonne, you need to stop. In this family we respect personal boundaries." If she continued, Dad could step between the kids.

Clarify which items belong to the child and which to the family. Anger often develops when children are forced to share items they believe belong to them alone. Circle the items your children may chose whether or not they wish to share:

new book	doll or old toys	trike or bike
red sweater	Halloween candy	pencils or erasers
food on plate	sports equipment	hats
blocks	bed for guest's nap	outgrown books

Develop procedures for passing items on. In some families the children go through their clothes and toys each summer and pass down items they have outgrown. Other families do this on each child's birthday. Any approach is okay as long as the children participate in the decision on which items to give up.

Help children maintain their boundaries. With very young children (less than three years old), you will need to monitor the boundaries yourself. Teach children your family rules and model different ways to handle situations.

With older preschoolers, act more like a coach and less like an enforcer. Go with the child to the situation and offer specific words and ideas he may use. You may have the children re-do the conflict from the beginning in a more constructive manner.

With school-aged children you need to begin to turn boundary conflicts over to them. Give them tools to handle situations and act as a resource or consultant. When kids have a problem, ask what they have tried before offering advice. However, remember that the safety of the children, whatever their ages, is always the parent's responsibility.

Using the STAR parenting process: Boundaries for Maria & Rosa

Stop & focus. When they fight over the doll, their mother Maria Elena might say to herself, "Maria and Rosa are still little. They are just beginning to learn about property rights. I need to protect them while I teach them about boundaries. I want Maria to wait for permission, and I would like Rosa to let Maria use her things occasionally."

Think of ideas. Some ideas Maria Elena might think of are:

- *Avoid the problem.* Get another doll for Maria.
- *Reduce stress.* Make sure you, as parent, get enough rest so you can remain patient and helpful.
- *Shaping with small steps.* Think, "First, I would like Maria to learn to ask for something and then to learn to wait for it."
- *Praise Maria when she asks.* Say, "Maria, I noticed you asked Rosa if you could use her doll."

- *Notice Rosa's improvement.* Say, "Rosa, that was kind of you to let Maria hold your doll for a minute."
- *Acknowledge Maria's feelings.* "Maria, I'll bet you feel frustrated that you can't play with Rosa's doll."
- *Explain the rule.* "You must get permission before you use someone else's toy."
- *Clarify limits.* "If you take Rosa's doll without permission, I will give the doll back to Rosa."
- *Follow through.* Give Rosa back her doll.
- *Offer two yeses.* Tell Maria, "That doll is Rosa's. You may wait until she will let you use it, or come and play with me."
- *Teach Rosa to trade.* Say, "Rosa, when Maria grabs your doll, get something else you think she will like. Then trade for your doll. If you need ideas, come ask me."
- *Model desired behavior.* When Rosa uses your pen say, "Rosa, that is my special pen. I will get you another one."

Act effectively. Maria Elena might think, "First, I want Maria to know that there are some things that aren't hers. She must ask for them and then respect the answer. I will remind her of our family rules and then praise her when she asks."

Review & revise. "I have to remember that the process of learning to respect boundaries takes time. If my plan does not work, I will try to model asking for things and give two yeses."

Using the STAR parenting process: Boundaries for Eddie & Devonne

Stop & focus. Dad might think, "Devonne deliberately destroyed Eddie's tower. She needs to respect boundaries even when she's bored. Eddie needs to learn how to deal with provoking behavior."

Think of ideas. Dad might consider ideas for both children:

- *Offer two yeses.* Say, "Devonne, respect Eddie's space. When you feel restless you may find something to do yourself or ask me for ideas."
- *Clarify limits.* "It's okay to feel bored. It's not okay to destroy Eddie's building."
- *Clarify a family rule.* Tell Devonne, "You are responsible for what your body does—accident or not."
- *Establish consequences.* "If you damage something, you must fix it as best you can." In this case, Devonne must help Eddie rebuild his tower.
- *Praise improvement.* When Devonne does not violate Eddie's boundary, say, "I noticed you took care of your feelings, without involving Eddie."
- *Reward good behavior.* Tell Devonne, "When you are in control of yourself enough to stay out of Eddie's space all afternoon and evening, you may stay up half an hour later."
- *Help Eddie avoid the problem.* Suggest that he build in the corner, rather than near the doorway.
- *Acknowledge Eddie's feelings.* "You must feel angry that Devonne knocked your tower down."
- *Grant in fantasy.* Say, "Wouldn't it be fun if you had a magic force field. Then no matter what Devonne did, she couldn't bother your buildings."
- *Teach Eddie to resolve issues with Devonne.* When Devonne provokes Eddie, suggest he tell her calmly what she did and what he wants her to do. For example, he might say, "Devonne, you knocked down my tower. You don't like it when I mess with your things. I want you to apologize."
- *Notice when Eddie speaks calmly.* Dad might say, "Eddie, I noticed how calmly you asked Devonne to apologize."

Act effectively. Dad might think, "I have two problems. Devonne needs to act responsibly. And, Eddie would do better to respond more wisely. I think I will begin by requiring Devonne to help Eddie rebuild his tower."

Review & revise. "If things are not better in a week, I will set up a system to reward Devonne for respecting boundaries. And I will teach Eddie to resolve conflicts with Devonne."

Using the STAR parenting process: Boundaries for Calvin & Erica

Stop & focus. Mom might think, "Calvin was respecting boundaries but Erica was not. I want to recognize Calvin's effort and teach Erica to respect people's bodies."

Think of ideas.

- *Avoid the problem.* Assign Erica a task in a different room.
- *Praise effort.* Say, "Calvin, you tried two ways to keep your feet safe. That was good thinking.
- *Change things.* Move the TV to Calvin's room so he can watch TV in peace.
- *Reduce stress.* Take Erica running before Calvin comes home from school. That will reduce her energy level.
- *Clarify limits.* Say, "Erica, in this family we respect personal boundaries. It is not okay to poke someone when they say, 'Stop.'"
- *Establish consequences.* "If you continue to bother Calvin after he says 'Stop,' you will need to do a kindness for him."
- *Notice Erica's good behavior.* Say, "I notice you stopped poking Calvin as soon as he asked you to."
- *Reward good behavior.* "Erica, today we are going to

practice stopping. When you stop the first time Calvin asks you, come and tell me. I will give you a star. When you have five stars, we can make pudding for dessert." Tomorrow you can reward Erica for stopping when she notices Calvin doesn't like being poked.

- *Model desired behavior.* Tickle Erica and stop immediately when she says, "Stop." Comment, "You said 'Stop,' and I stopped immediately."
- *Acknowledge Calvin's feelings.* "It's frustrating to try to watch TV when someone is poking you."
- *Teach Calvin more skills.* Suggest he try asking Erica what she wants. For example, "Erica, I asked you to stop. You want me to stop when I tickle you. Why are you poking me?"

Act effectively. Mom might think, "Erica is bothering Calvin more. I want to stop that behavior quickly. I will tell her to do Calvin the kindness of setting the table for him when she ignores his request to stop. I will also look for times when she stops at his first request. I will encourage Calvin by commenting when I see him use two strategies."

Review & revise. "I will try this for five days. If Erica's behavior continues to increase, I will try rewarding her efforts to stop, and I'll teach Calvin more ways to respond to provoking behavior."

Wise words

One of the best ways to help children understand their boundaries is to be clear about your own boundaries.

If you have trouble maintaining your personal boundaries, get someone to help you figure out why. Talk with a friend, relative, or counselor. It may be that your boundaries were ignored as a child. Or it may be that you are too tired to cope. Or you might not know what to do. The guidelines presented here are useful for parents as well as for children.

Remember to change your approach as your children grow older. Begin by enforcing boundaries with young children. Then act as coach, offering words and strategies for them to use. Then pull back to the role of consultant. If you continue to enforce your children's boundaries for them as they grow older, they may depend on you to fight their battles, rather than developing their own skills.

Give kids five people they can go to for help. Children need people they can turn to when parents are gone or unresponsive. The people should be ones who will listen nonjudgmentally and offer the child support. These people can be aunt, uncle, grandparent, neighbor, a friend's parent, school teacher, religious school teacher, etc. They can be resources for general concerns as well as sibling issues.

Skill 3
Dealing with feelings

Martin, age $2^1/_2$, wanted the truck his twin brother Michael was playing with. Martin pointed and said, "Mine." When Michael didn't give him the truck, Martin got angry and hit Michael.

"I want to go, too! Why can't I go?" Anthony, age $4^1/_2$, wailed as he watched his older brother James pack for a weekend camping trip. "I know," Anthony announced, "Dad can take me."

James explained again, "You can't go camping unless you are a member of the troop. And Dad is one of the scout leaders, so he has to go."

When James left to find his boots, Anthony took James's flashlight and hid it. Then he quietly left the room.

Devonne, age 10, was tired of reading. She was tired of drawing, beading, watching TV, and doing homework. She didn't want to clean her room or help her mom.

She watched her brother Eddie smile as he built a tall tower. She picked up her book and headed for the door. As she passed her brother, the book slipped from her hand and demolished his building.

Eddie screamed, "You broke my tower! You poopy-head!"

Feelings enrich life. However, when you have two or more children, feelings also complicate life. The previous situations illustrate several different feelings. Martin is envious. Michael is angry. James is excited that he is going camping. Anthony feels disappointed that he can't go. Devonne feels bored. Eddie felt pleased and then feels angry.

What children need to know about feelings

Siblings need information about feelings. When children understand feelings, they can begin to respond to them appropriately. Children need a feeling vocabulary. They need to know that feelings change. They need to know the difference between feelings and actions. And they also need various strategies for dealing with feelings.

A "feeling" vocabulary. Children need to know words to describe their feelings and other people's. They need words for both comfortable feelings (happy, excited) and uncomfortable feelings (angry, frustrated, bored). They also need words for a range of feelings from mild to intense. For example, tentative/scared/ petrified; contented/happy/elated; or annoyed/angry/livid. When children can name feelings, they can begin to think about them more effectively.

Feelings are neither good nor bad. Feelings are emotions. Emotions are tools that give kids information. They might tell kids a place is safe or unsafe, a person means well or is harmful, an activity is fun or dangerous.

When you deny a feeling ("You're not mad at Uncle Max, you know he didn't mean to hurt you.") or discount a feeling ("Don't make such a big deal. It's only a tiny ow-ie.") you teach children to mistrust their feelings. When they mistrust their feelings they lose a valuable tool for dealing with themselves and other people.

Feelings change. Most children live in the present. Martin was afraid he would never get a turn with the truck. Anthony was disappointed that he would be left behind. When children feel angry or lonely they believe they will always feel that way. When they realize that feelings change, children can begin to control their feelings.

Feelings are different from actions. Feelings are inside the body. Actions are outside. Actions are what kids do or say. When Martin felt angry, he chose to hit Michael. He could have felt mad and stamped his feet or called Dad for help instead of hitting. Feelings can be responded to in many different ways.

There are many ways to express feelings. Some ways are helpful. Other ways hurt either the child or someone else. For example, Martin hit Michael. Anthony hid James's flashlight. Eddie screamed.

Children need several constructive ways to deal with feelings. One of the most effective ways is to calm down. When children are very upset, it is hard for them to think about the consequences of their actions. They think more clearly when they feel calm. Read the list of ideas on page 47 and check the ways you might like your child to calm himself or herself.

Moving	**Sound**	**Thinking**
run in place	sing a mad song	visualize yourself in a calm place
stamp a foot	talk to someone	imagine the feeling melting away
squish playdough	listen to marching music	think "I can handle this."
take deep breaths	listen to calm music	
throw a ball		

Comforting	**Creative**	**Humorous**
read a book	make up a poem	draw a silly picture
take a bath	draw a picture	tell jokes
get a hug	play drums	make silly rhymes
call a friend	tear newspaper	look for humor in the situation

Some children discover calming techniques by themselves. Other children need to be taught. Once a child knows how to calm himself, you may need to find ways to encourage him to use those techniques.

Parent's role

The parent's role is as coach. Watch your children's behavior and observe their problems, then decide how to help the siblings gain the skills they need. You can help children in several ways.

Use "feeling" words. Label your feelings. Reflect your children's feelings. This will give them language to discuss how they are feeling before they act.

Label your feelings. "I am annoyed that you kids are arguing while I'm trying to balance the checkbook." Or, "I'm pleased you offered your sister some marking pens."

Reflect children's feelings. "You felt impatient waiting to play with the truck." Or, "You're disappointed you can't go on the camping trip."

Distinguish between feelings and behavior. Remind children that any feeling is okay. However, actions that hurt people or things are not okay. For example, you might say to Martin, "It's okay to feel frustrated, but it's not okay to hit Michael." Or you might say to Devonne, "Looks to me like you're bored. You need to find a more appropriate way to deal with boredom."

Clarify limits. Remind the child of the family rule and the consequence. For example, "Touch gently. If you can't touch gently, then play alone or do a kindness."

Teach skills to deal with feelings. When people are angry they need skills to calm themselves and skills to deal with the problem. In the next section we will look at how several families deal with feelings. Problem-solving skills follow in the next chapter.

Using the STAR parenting process: Dealing with Martin's anger

Stop & focus. Paul, Martin's father, might say to himself, "Martin is 2½. He is beginning to learn people skills. He needs a lot of help dealing with feelings. Since he is very physical, he needs some physical ways to deal with his feelings. Since his developmental task is to learn about feelings, I will focus on teaching him about feelings."

Think of ideas. Some possible ideas Paul might consider are:

- *Model calming down.* When Paul is mad he might say, "I'm really angry. I'm going to take a vigorous walk right now. When I get back, I'll think about what I can do."
- *Teach a calming tool.* Sit beside Martin and show him

how to blow out angry feelings by taking deep breaths.

- *Clarify the rule.* Tell him, "It is okay to be angry. And you need to find another way to get the truck."
- *Give him two yeses.* Say, "Martin, when you want a toy you may ask or trade for it."
- *Reflect Martin's feelings.* "You feel angry that Michael won't give you the truck right now."
- *Notice good behavior.* When Martin tries to act appropriately, say, "Martin, I noticed you asked Michael for the truck. I'll bet you're proud of yourself for asking."
- *Avoid the problem.* Physical exercise reduces anger build-up. Go for a walk before supper with Martin to make sure he gets enough physical exercise each day.
- *Re-do it right.* Next time Martin gets angry and hits say, "Oops, you forgot to take deep breaths." Then sit down beside him and model taking deep breaths.

Act effectively. Paul might decide, "I think I will try teaching Martin to calm himself before he acts. At first, I'll sit down beside him and take big breaths. Then, I'll watch to see when he uses breaths and congratulate him. If he hits Michael, I'll go over and ask him to re-do it right with me."

Review & revise. "I'll try this for five days. Then I'll show Martin a different way to calm himself. I also need to remember Michael and praise him for touching gently and using his words, so he doesn't start hitting to get attention."

Using the STAR parenting process: Dealing with Anthony's disappointment

Stop & focus. Angela, Anthony's mom, might have guessed what happened when James couldn't find his flashlight and accused Anthony of taking it. She might think, "Anthony is upset again. But at least things are getting better; he didn't hit and he didn't break anything. I guess we have to work on disappointment now."

Think of ideas. Some ideas Angela might think of are:

- *Reflect Anthony's feelings.* She might say, "You're really disappointed that James is going camping and you're not."
- *Clarify family rules.* "It's okay to be disappointed. But it's not okay to hide James's things. You can find another way to express your feelings."
- *Give two yeses.* "It's not okay to hide other people's belongings. When you are disappointed you can find something fun to do or you can talk to someone about how you feel."
- *Notice improvement.* Angela might say, "Anthony, I noticed you were upset, and you remembered not to hit. You're gaining self-control." Note: To be effective Angela will need to avoid commenting on misbehavior at the same time.
- *Avoid the problem.* She could arrange some fun activity for Anthony so he might not be as disappointed.
- *Model dealing with feelings.* "I'm sad Dad and Anthony are going camping. I'll miss them. And I'm going to play a lot of jazz music this weekend because Dad doesn't like it and I really do. The jazz won't irritate him when he's gone."
- *Teach Anthony to think positively.* She could say, "James is going camping for the weekend. You can feel disappointed that you are not going, or happy that we will have some special time alone together."
- *Remind Anthony he is in charge of his feelings.* "You can decide if you want to stay disappointed or you want to feel happy. Feelings can change if you let them. It's your choice."

Act effectively. Angela might decide to encourage Anthony to be in charge of his feelings, rather than planning something fun for them to do herself. She could begin by acknowledging his feelings, and sharing what she did in a similar situation. She could finish by reminding him he is in charge of his feelings.

Review & revise. Angela could review the situation the next day. If Anthony were still disappointed, she could clarify his choice and offer help. "I see you still want to be upset. If you want to change your feelings, you can ask me for ideas."

Using the STAR parenting process: Dealing with Devonne's boredom

Stop & focus. Belinda, Devonne's mother, might think, "Oh, she's at it again. I wish she wouldn't pick on Eddie when she's bored."

Think of ideas. Ideas Belinda might consider are:

- *Reflect Devonne's feelings.* She might say, "Devonne, looks to me like you're bored."
- *Clarify options.* "You can find something constructive to do, or I can find something for you to do."
- *Give two yeses.* "You can put your restless energy to work or make a list of all the things you might do if you didn't feel bored."
- *Clarify family rules.* "Deal with your own distress, don't spread it around."
- *Clarify another family rule.* "You are responsible for what your body does—accident or not."
- *Avoid the problem.* Enroll Devonne in swimming class, and let her swim off some of her energy.
- *Notice a constructive change.* Notice when she gets interested in something and comment on how clever

she was to find something to do.

- *Model changing your feelings.* Belinda could say, "I'm so tired of housework. I don't want to do anything that needs to be done. I think I'll do some aerobics and see if I feel better."
- *Reward progress.* Tell Devonne, "Each hour you find constructive outlets for your feelings, you may have a bongo buck. When you have ten bongo bucks we can go buy you some new pastels."

Act effectively. Belinda might think, "I guess I am going to have to deal with the boredom directly. I'll let the behavior pass for the moment. I think I'll model dealing with my boredom. I'll remind her to handle her own feelings, and ask her whether she wants to stay bored or feel something different."

Review & revise. "If this plan doesn't work, I'll reward Devonne with bongo bucks when she expresses her feelings constructively."

Wise words

Review each child's developmental task. Adjust your expectations to reflect your child's developmental stage and temperament.

Martin, age 2½, has the primary task of understanding feelings. He needs lots of help and coaching on separating feelings from actions.

Anthony, age 4½, is beginning to separate feelings from actions. He needs more support on looking at positive options for expressing his feelings.

Devonne, age 10, has a lot of tools and needs to be encouraged to use them. Remember that some children's emotional development does not match their age.

Put your children in charge of their feelings. Parents are often tempted to discount children's feelings or to try to fix them by solving the problem for the children. Neither approach helps children.

Discounting. "That doesn't matter. Devonne really likes you."

"Don't screech. You can build a new tower."

Fixing. "Don't cry. I'll help you rebuild the tower."

"Don't be upset, Anthony. You and I can do something really special."

Handle your own feelings. If the kids' behavior bothers you, tell them how you feel when the behavior occurs. The kids' behavior may not change, but you will be modeling constructive ways to express feelings.

Poor modeling. "You kids make me so mad. I can't think when you make so much noise." Parent puts kids in charge of his feelings.

Helpful modeling. "I feel mad when I need quiet and my kids are quarreling." Parent accepts responsibility for his own feelings.

Get outside help. Anger from a current problem can usually be redirected. If you or your child have a lot of angry feelings that are not helped by these ideas, get outside help. Unresolved anger from previous situations of helplessness or abuse may need professional help to be resolved.

Getting help when you need it is a sign of competence rather than failure. It's like going to the doctor with a broken arm, rather than trying to set the bone yourself.

Feelings are tied to situations. Children need tools to handle both the feelings and the situations. We have looked at ways to deal with feelings. Next we will look at strategies to deal with the situation or problem.

Skill 4
Solving problems

Devonne, age 10, was tired of reading. She was tired of drawing, beading, watching TV, and doing homework. She didn't want to clean her room or help her mom.

She watched Eddie, age $4\frac{1}{2}$, build a tall tower. Then she picked up her book and headed for the door. As she passed her brother, the book slipped from her hand and demolished his building.

Eddie screamed, "You broke my tower!"

Devonne replied smugly, "It was an accident."

Maria, age $2\frac{1}{2}$, wanted Rosa's doll. When Rosa, age $3\frac{1}{2}$, put it down for a moment, Maria grabbed it. Rosa screeched, "Give it to me!" Maria ignored her, and a battle over the doll began again.

Calvin, age 9, was sitting on the sofa watching a video. Erica, age 4, came over and started poking his feet. He told her to quit it. She giggled and continued. He tucked his feet under him to protect them. Then Erica tried to push him over. She lost her balance, slipped off the sofa, and hurt her head.

Everyone has power. Each person may chose to use his or her power or give it away by not using it.

People may use power constructively or destructively. Constructive use of power promotes learning and growth. Destructive use of power hurts people and encourages them to rebel or to stay stuck.

What children need to know about power

There are two types of power. These are positional power and personal power. Positional power is power *over other people.* Personal power is each person's power *over herself.*

Positional power. Positional power comes from your role. Parents have positional power over their children; teachers over their students; a boss over his or her employees. A teen-aged babysitter has positional power over the children she cares for. Positional power ends when the relationship that created it ends. A boss with no employee has no positional power. A babysitter has positional power only while she babysits.

Personal power. Personal power is the ability to act or respond to the events in your life. Everyone has personal power; however, some people do not use it. Personal power is based on a secure knowledge of who you are as a person and your ability to make clear, thoughtful decisions.

When Eddie lets Marty scribble on his drawing without

asking him to stop or moving away, he gives up his personal power in the situation. When Alexandra does not try out for a part in a play she wants because she is afraid she won't get it, she reduces her personal power. When Suzo decides to ask the principal for help dealing with bullies on the bus, she is using her personal power.

Personal power comes from looking at what you want, considering your options, and acting. Sometimes people act by themselves. Other times they need to get help or support from other people. Personal power involves reviewing your options and deciding how to use the resources you have: knowledge, friends, physical build, money, energy, etc. Interestingly, it is the ability to use what is at hand that makes a person powerful.

People use power in different ways. Everyone has personal power and some people have positional power, as well. People use their power in different ways.

Coercive power. Some people have the power to compel someone to do something. This may be because of their physical size or the position they hold. Coercive power can be kind, as when a parent snatches a child from the street. Or it can be hurtful, as when a parent beats a child for misbehaving. Coercive power, whether by a bully, a parent, or a bureaucrat, eventually causes fear, or resentment, or resistance regardless of how well intended its use is.

Persuasive power. Some people use gentle or indirect methods to get people to do what they want. They may coax, reason, lie, trick, beg, reward, bribe, or appear helpless to get what they want.

Persuasive power may be used constructively (to motivate) or destructively (to manipulate). Power is constructive when it motivates a person to do something in his or her best interest. Coaxing a sick child to take his medicine or rewarding a teen for quitting smoking are in the best interest of the person being influenced.

Persuasive power is destructive when it manipulates

people in ways that reduce trust or decrease self-esteem. When a parent promises a treat in exchange for cooperation and fails to follow through, a child feels lied to. People who have been manipulated feel anger or resentment when they realize how they were used.

Cooperative power. Cooperative power is shared power. Whether the participants are equal or unequal, each person's needs are considered. Cooperative power finds solutions that work for both people. The process may be as simple as offering choices, or as complicated as extensive negotiation.

No one has complete control. Many young children want to control their worlds. They get angry when rain cancels a desired activity, a friend can't come over, or a pet dies. Kids may scream loudly or strike out wildly, but they still have no control. Children need to learn that they cannot control everything.

Children always have choices. Children may not be able to control all the situations in life, but they can control how they respond to the situations. This is the essence of personal power. The choice may be as simple as accepting the inevitable or fighting it.

In most cases, however, kids can use the tools discussed in establishing boundaries, or the problem-solving process described on pages 60–61 to work things out. Parents should remind kids that if they can't solve problems themselves, they can ask a grown-up for help.

Sometimes the quick solution backfires. In the example of Maria, Rosa, and the doll, both sisters wanted the doll. Maria grabbed the doll as soon as she could, but Rosa returned and grabbed it back. When Mom heard the noises she came and put the doll up. Maria and Rosa's quick solution, grabbing the doll, backfired. Neither child could play with the doll as a result.

Parent's role

Clarify who has power over the sibling. Parents have positional power over their child. However, in some families, an older child may also have positional power over his siblings. This happens when parents expect an older sibling to watch out for younger siblings. Other families feel that it is the parents' job, not a child's, to be responsible for siblings. Each family must decide and clarify who has positional power over whom.

Distinguish between negotiable and non-negotiable rules. Negotiable rules encourage problem solving and cooperation. The parent listens to the children's concerns and discusses how both their needs may be met. Non-negotiable rules must be obeyed promptly, as with safety issues. However, even non-negotiable rules may be revised when needed. Children need *both* negotiable and non-negotiable rules.

Model using cooperative power. Children learn more by what parents do than by what they say. You can model negotiation two ways with your partner or your child.

With your partner. If you have a conflict with your partner, model negotiating your differences. Begin with a simple problem and then move to more complex ones. You can use the STAR process as illustrated on pages 18–21.

With your child. If you want children to find cooperative solutions, then you need to spend some time modeling behavior that considers kids' needs. Use "A better way," two yeses, or the STAR process to problem solve with your child. Avoid the temptation to use coercive power because modeling coercive power makes it more attractive to kids.

Model negotiation with partner

Stop & focus. Say to your spouse, "I noticed you want to use the car tomorrow to go to the library and research your paper. I was planning to go to the PTA meeting. What are our options?"

Think of ideas. Dad goes tonight. Mom gets a ride to the PTA meeting. Get a babysitter and drop Dad at the library during the PTA meeting, etc.

Act effectively. Chose an idea with your spouse. Dad might agree to go to the library tonight.

Review & revise. The next night at dinner, Mom might ask Dad, "Did going to the library last night work all right for you?"

Help children identify the kinds of power others use. You can look for different kinds of power in books, on television, and in real life.

Television & video. When you watch *Beauty & the Beast* you could ask, "What kind of power does Gaston use to convince Bella to marry him?"

Books. When you read *King of the Playground* ask, "What kind of power did Sammy use to keep Kevin from playing in the sand box?"

Real situations. When a guest grabs a toy from the toddler, ask, "What kind of power is he using to get the truck?"

Expand the discussion by asking, "How did the other people in the story feel about that use of power?" or "What else could the character have tried to get what he wanted?"

Give kids skills to handle power conflicts. With some conflicts the problem is the issue; with other conflicts, power is the issue.

When the problem is the issue, children can use the problem-solving steps to deal with the situation. Both the steps and how to facilitate them are described on pages 60–61.

When power is the issue, give your child a strategy to deal with destructive or hurtful power. This is presented on page 63.

Steps in solving problems

Here are five steps kids can use to solve problems now and as adults. You will notice that this process is very similar to the STAR process we suggested earlier (pages 18–21). The only difference is that this process divides the "Stop and focus" step into two parts: "Calm yourself" and "Identify the problem."

In this example, we assume that Calvin is familiar with the problem-solving process, and can use it himself.

1. Calm yourself. It is difficult to think of good ideas when you are upset. For ways to calm yourself, see page 47.

When Erica pokes Calvin he might say, "I am not going to let that twerp bug me. I will count to ten and then think about what to do."

2. Identify the problem. Decide what you want. Find out what the other person wants.

Calvin might think, "I want to watch TV . . . I'm not sure what Erica wants. She's not messing with the controls so it's probably not the TV she wants. When I asked her to quit, she giggled. Maybe it's ME she wants to play with."

He might ask, "Erica, do you want to play with me?"

She might nod her head.

Then he might think, "I have a problem. I want to watch the video, and she wants to play with me."

3. Think of ideas. Find several different ideas. Some can be silly ideas. Silly ideas often spark good ideas.

Calvin might think, "If I don't do anything she will continue to bug me. I could tell Mom she's a pest. I could poke her back. I could let her look at my new book as long as she lets me watch the video. I could turn her into a kitten and play with her while I watch. I could ask her to watch with me, if she were quiet."

4. Act effectively. Consider the ideas. Decide where to start and make a plan.

Calvin might think, "If I ask Mom, she'll say, 'Solve it yourself.' I really don't want Erica to play with my book. I'm afraid she might mess it up. I can't make her a cat, but I could ask her to sit with me. I'll do it. If that doesn't work I can try asking Mom or I can make a deal about the book."

5. Review & revise. Look back at what you did. Did it work? If it didn't, try another idea. Keep going until you find something that works.

At the end of the video Calvin might think, "I did it. I figured out a way to watch the video. It wasn't so bad. Next time I might ask her if she wants to watch with me."

Steps in helping kids negotiate

The problem-solving process shown above can also be used by two children to resolve their differences. Before children can learn to generate ideas and evaluate them, they need certain skills. They need to be able to listen, to pay attention, and to understand some emotional concepts. This usually happens between ages three and four.

In the beginning, a parent may need to facilitate the discussion between children. Your role is to provide the structure in which children work out their differences. Avoid the temptation to suggest ideas or influence the decision the children make. As siblings become more skilled with the process they can begin to work by themselves.

1. Ask siblings to try problem solving together. For example, say to your children Noriko (4) and Takeo (6), "Let's sit down and see if you two can work this out together."

2. Help siblings frame the issue neutrally. "Noriko wants to watch *Sesame Street.* Takeo wants to watch *Where in the World Is Carmen Sandiego?* And both shows start at four o'clock. How can you plan things so you both will be happy?"

3. Encourage lots of different ideas. Once children are familiar with the process ask them to find at least one idea per year of age. (A three-year-old thinks of three ideas. A six-year-old thinks of six ideas.) Tell the kids some ideas can be silly.

Focus on kids' ideas. When children are thinking of ideas resist the temptation to offer your own ideas. If you introduce ideas children often assume their ideas are not as good as yours and they lose interest in the problem-solving process.

4. Ask for a decision that will work for both siblings. Read the list of ideas and ask, "Noriko, what idea do you think would work for both you and Takeo?" If Noriko has no ideas you can ask Takeo. Check that the ideas will work with the other sibling. For example, "Takeo, does Noriko's idea work for you?" If the idea doesn't help, ask the children to revise it so it will.

5. Review the decision with the siblings. Ask, "Did the idea you tried work? Did it feel fair to both of you?"

Introduce more ideas between conflicts. Children often have the same conflict again and again. This is, in part, because they are trying to understand and feel powerful. You can introduce new ideas in several ways:

- Read the *Children's Problem Solving Books.*
- Model a new problem-solving idea.
- Wonder, "What might have happened if . . ."
- Notice what children at the park or in the mall do.
- Share how you resolved a similar issue as a child.
- Make a family idea list. Write down the children's

ideas and encourage them to add more ideas as they think of them.

Steps in dealing with hurtful power

Children need help dealing with hurtful power. People who use coercive or persuasive power do so because they want something physical, some action, or a sense of power. One strategy is to remain in control of yourself, even if you cannot control the situation. Five steps are described below.

1. Center yourself. Take a deep breath, count to ten, look out the window, imagine the other person covered with slime, stand evenly on both feet, or do whatever you can to calm yourself.

2. Clarify the situation. This may involve stating clearly what happened or asking a question to help the other person focus attention on the situation.

3. State your wishes. Clarify for yourself or others what you would like to see happen. The request can be fanciful, humorous, or practical.

4. Request action. Be specific. Invite, not demand, the other person to help resolve the situation he or she created. When you demand, the other person usually becomes more fixed in his or her position.

5. Review your choices. At this point you have these three ways to maintain your boundaries:

- Negotiate
- Move, or
- Get help

It is not always possible for children to resolve conflicts. Remind them to get support if they are bullied or threatened. Bullies are a grown-up's problem. Children should not be expected to solve issues of violence or intimidation alone.

Problem solving and dealing with hurtful power conflicts are complex skills. These skills are learned slowly over time. In general, problem-solving ability begins between

Solving power problems

	Coercive power Devonne knocked Eddie's block tower down.	**Manipulative power** Juan taunts, "Lupita is a baby. Lupita is a baby."
1. Center yourself	Eddie could take three deep breaths and remind himself, "I can decide how to respond."	Lupita might count to five and say, "I am in charge of me."
2. Clarify the situation	"You deliberately knocked my block tower down."	"Why do you like chanting that?" (Juan, "It's fun.")
3. State wishes	"I wish you would deal with your problems rather than dumping them on me."	"Well, I wish you spoke French so I had no idea what you were saying."
4. Request action	"Will you help me rebuild the tower?" (Devonne, "No!")	"Would you like to play a board game together?" (Juan, "No.")
5. Review choices	Try moving: "Okay, I'll build in my room."	Try problem solving: "Well, what would you like to do?"

three and six years, and dealing with hurtful power conflicts begins in elementary school.

We will now look at how parents could handle specific problems.

Using the STAR parenting process: Problem solving with Maria & Rosa

Stop & focus. Maria Elena, the girls' mother, might think, "Maria and Rosa are quite young. I need to teach them skills so that when they are older they will be able to solve problems themselves. I want to start by showing Maria how to ask and how to trade. I want to show Rosa how to keep her things out of Maria's reach."

Think of ideas.

- *Avoid the problem.* Give Rosa a shelf where she can put her doll up out of Maria's reach.
- *Teach new skills.* For example, when Maria reaches for Rosa's toy, stop and say, "Maria, that is Rosa's doll. Ask her if you may use it.
- *Reduce stress.* Make sure the girls get enough exercise.
- *Shaping.* Teach the idea of trading. (See below.)

How to teach trading

1. Model trading. "Maria, let's see if Rosa will trade for this."
2. Give Maria a toy you think Rosa will like and tell Maria to trade.
3. Offer Maria two toys and ask her to choose which one she thinks Rosa will like.
4. Offer Maria three toys and ask her to choose one for Rosa.
5. Finally, ask Maria to find a toy Rosa will like.

(Note: you may need to repeat each step of the process several times.)

- *Praise desired behavior.* Say, "Maria, I noticed that you asked. That's one way to get what you want."
- *Notice improvement.* When Maria watches Rosa play with a toy and then asks for it, praise her.
- *Change things.* Remove items that the girls have most conflict over and let Rosa play with them while Maria naps.
- *Offer two yeses.* Say, "No grabbing. You may trade or ask."
- *Reward good behavior.* Say, "Maria, I noticed you asked to use Rosa's doll and she said, 'Later.' I'll play with you a bit while you wait." (Parent's playing rewards waiting.)
- *Model desired behavior.* When you come in from outside say to Rosa, "I have to remember to put my purse up high so Maria won't be tempted to get into it."
- *Acknowledge feelings.* "It's frustrating to wait for something you want."
- *Make a rule.* "Ask before you use things that belong to others."
- *Establish consequences.* Say, "If you take someone's toy without asking, you must immediately give it back." With older preschoolers (four or five years old) you might want to add that they need to do a kindness.
- *Follow through.* When kids take something without asking, remind them to give it back. For example, "You need to give that back to Rosa. Do you want to do it yourself or do you want me to help you?"

Act effectively. Mom might think, "I really want to concentrate on teaching new skills. I know Maria is too young to negotiate right now, so I will teach her to ask and trade for what she wants. I will look for improvement and praise her when I see it. When she grabs I will offer two yeses.

I will encourage Rosa to put her things up when she is not using them. To make that easier, I'll clean off a shelf of the bookshelves in the living room so that she can put her things there temporarily."

Review & revise. "I'll try this for a week. If Maria doesn't improve, I will reward her *efforts* more clearly."

Using the STAR parenting process: Power issues with Calvin & Erica

Stop & focus. Mom might think, "Calvin and Erica have a lot of conflicts around the TV. They need to learn to work some of their hassles out together. I will teach Calvin and Erica to negotiate."

Think of ideas.

- *Change things.* Remove the TV. Put it in a closet where it can't be used.
- *Avoid the problem.* Invite a friend over for Erica.
- *Teach new skills.* Introduce the problem-solving process by reading *I Want It* or *I Want to Play (Children's Problem Solving Books)* to Calvin and Erica.
- *Model desired behavior.* Use the STAR process to model negotiation at the dinner table. (See pages 58–59.)
- *Offer two yeses.* "If you want something, you can negotiate or you can wait."
- *Praise effort.* "Erica, you asked Calvin if you could sit by him. That was thoughtful of you."
- *Notice improvement.* Say, "Calvin, I noticed you thinking about what to do when Erica poked your feet."
- *Reward negotiation.* Each time they try, they will each get one marble to put in the jar. When they find a solution they like, give them each three marbles. When the jar is filled, have a family treat.
- *Acknowledge Calvin's feelings.* Say, "It sure is frustrating when you want to concentrate and someone bothers you."
- *Reflect Erica's feelings.* "You feel ignored. I'll bet you wish Calvin would play with you."

- *Make a rule.* "Touch gently."
- *Clarify limits.* Remind Erica, "Touch gently or play in your room."
- *Follow through.* If she continues to bother Calvin, say, "I see you have chosen to play in your room. Do you want to go yourself or do you want me to help?" If she doesn't go, say, "I see you want help."

Act effectively. Mom might think, "Erica is 4. She is old enough to begin to use negotiation to get what she wants. I will teach her the problem-solving process by reading the *Children's Problem Solving Books.* Then I will help the kids use the problem-solving process to find an effective solution.

Review & revise. "I will evaluate the progress in a week. If the kids still do not cooperate, I will reward each of them for *trying.* When the jar is filled with marbles we will go to the zoo together."

Using the STAR parenting process: Power issues with Eddie & Devonne

Stop & focus. Dad might think, "Eddie and Devonne have had conflicts like this before. Eddie knows that the doorway is not a wise place to build. Devonne also knows that she needs to deal with her feelings, not dump them on others. I think I need to help them work conflicts out. I will focus on Devonne since she is older and has more experience."

Think of ideas.

- *Avoid the problem.* Say, "Devonne, you are a powerful person. You can find a way to have excitement that doesn't hurt anyone."
- *Reduce stress.* Go running with Devonne each day to help reduce background stress.

- *Offer two yeses.* "When you are feeling irritable or bored, you can find a kind solution yourself or come talk to me."
- *Praise effort.* "I noticed you used your power constructively. When Eddie was bothering you, you went to your room."
- *Reward good behavior.* "If you are feeling bored and want to bake, come to me and we'll make cookies."
- *Model desired behavior.* Think of options within Devonne's hearing. Say, "I'm feeling irritable. What shall I do? Shall I turn off the TV the kids are watching? Demand the kids clean the living room right now? Run around the block to reduce my fidgets?"
- *Acknowledge feelings.* "Looks like you're feeling bored or restless."
- *Make a rule.* "You are responsible for what your body does—accident or not."
- *Clarify limits.* "If you damage something that belongs to someone else, you must repair the item.
- *Establish consequences.* "If you are unable or unwilling to repair the damage, then you must do a kindness for that person before you can do anything for yourself." The kindness could be doing a chore for Eddie, playing a game with him, letting him hold her special glass bird, or ____________.
- *Follow through.* When Devonne's friend comes over to play, tell the friend, "Devonne will be available as soon as she does a kindness for her brother."
- *Re-do it right.* Say, "Oops, you knocked down the tower. Let's build it up and then you can practice walking past it carefully."

Act effectively. "I want to affirm Devonne's power and channel it constructively. I will remind her that she is powerful, and give her two yeses. Then I will look for *effort* and praise it."

Review & revise. "I will record conflicts for two weeks. If things do not improve, I will focus on setting limits. I will remind Devonne of the rule, and see that she does a kindness when she misuses her power."

Wise words

Separate your power needs from those of your children. Sometimes parents have a very strong need to be in control. They expect children to obey them immediately. They cannot accept children's input or their needs. When parents' power needs are this strong, children either decide they are powerless, or that they will be powerful also, no matter what.

When children decide they are powerless, they are vulnerable to anyone with a strong personality and need for power. When children decide power is very important, they may rebel or become devious in using their power.

Insist on respectful use of power. Establish family rules for appropriate power use. Check the rules you want to adopt. Add additional rules that are important to you.

- *Touch gently.* You are responsible for what your body does.
- *Use words.* Tell others what is wrong and what you need.
- *Find win-win solutions.* Be sure everyone's needs are met.
- *Use positive power.* Build people up, don't tear them down.

Decide on consequences for children who disregard rules.

Consider developmental stage when responding to power conflicts. A child's task from three to six years old is to figure out his or her power relationship to others. Power conflicts with siblings and parents will usually be frequent as the child sorts out how to be powerful. Your task is to teach the child what you want him or her to know about power.

Children from six to twelve are learning about structure. They experiment to find out how things work in the larger world. This often involves bringing new ideas home and trying them out. Also, sometimes when children feel powerless in the larger world, they try to assert their power with siblings. Again, parents need to consider what they want children to learn, and then decide how to teach those concepts.

Share this book with a friend, neighbor, or relative who can be a support as you use the ideas. Set up regular times to share successes and brainstorm problems you encounter. Working with others can be fun and offers useful insights.

Solving your problems

You can use this worksheet to help you solve the sibling problems in your house. If you have questions, refer to the third chapter, on STAR parenting, or the examples for each task.

Describe in one sentence the behavior you want to focus on first.

Use the STAR process below to solve your problem. Remember, you may need to review results and revise your plan several times. Keep at it!

S — Stop & focus

Calm yourself enough to think clearly.
When the behavior occurs I feel ______________________
When I am upset with my child's behavior I will calm myself by
____

Is this really important? ____ *yes* ____ *no*

How frequently does the behavior happen?
It happens ______________________ *an hour, day, or week.*

What is the child's developmental task? (See chart, page 13.)
My child's developmental task is ______________________

What do I want my child to *do* instead?
I want my child to ______________________________

What skill does my child need to be more successful?
He or she needs __________________________________

T — Think of ideas

Find at least two ideas for each of the five points below. If you want ideas, look at the examples in "Think of ideas" (pages 27, 28, 38, 40, 41, 48, 50, 51, 65, 67, 68, and 69).

Teach new skills
Modeling ______________________________________
Shaping ______________________________________
Re-do it right __________________________________

Respond to cooperation
Attention ______________________________________
Praise ____
Rewards _______________________________________

Acknowledge feelings
Simple listening ______________________
Active listening ______________________
Grant in fantasy ______________________

Set limits
Clear rule ______________________
Consequence ______________________
A better way ______________________

Avoid problems
Give two yeses ______________________
Reduce stress ______________________
Change things ______________________

A — Act effectively

Choose one or two ideas to start with.
I will try ______________________
and ______________________

What do you need to do before you start?
Before I begin I need to ______________________

R — Review & revise

How long will you try these ideas?

____

What will you try next if these ideas don't work?

____
____
____

If you have revised your plan several times and the situation does not improve, you may need outside support. The next chapter will help you decide whether or not the problem is serious. Remember, there are solutions, though they may not be obvious and may take time to find.

When should you worry?

Michelle is so bossy. She tells everyone what to do. I'm afraid she won't have any friends when she gets to school.

My son Kirk gets furious with very little provocation. He gets so angry he strikes out at people. I'm afraid he is going to end up an axe murderer.

Willie won't let me out of his sight. If he can't see me he whimpers. I can't do anything without him clinging.

Asha is so selfish. She wants everything other kids have. And, she won't let anyone touch her toys. If someone even looks at them she will grab them away.

Normal children have challenging behavior.

A few normal children have very, very challenging behavior. Sometimes it is hard to tell the difference between "normal" challenging behavior and "serious" behavior.

The tools in this book will help you deal with normal developmental behavior problems. However, if the underlying cause is due to an organic problem, the family system, or personal stressors, you will probably need more help.

Five questions to ask yourself

How can you tell if your child will outgrow the behavior or needs professional help? There is no thermometer or lab test that can tell the future accurately. However, there are some questions that will help you decide. The more questions you answer "no" to, the more likely it is you have a problem that should be evaluated.

1. Has your child's temperament remained consistent? On page 16 we listed nine temperament traits that are consistent over time. If a child is persistent, active, intense, and grumpy, he or she will be more difficult than a child who is inactive, quiet, cheerful, and does not persist much.

If Kirk was physically active and intense as a baby, he will probably still be more intense and physical at 4 or 8 than other kids. However, if he was a quiet and mellow baby and toddler and is now intensely and aggressively angry you have cause for concern.

2. Is your child's behavior typical for his or her developmental stage? Two-year-olds have temper tantrums.

Kid's developmental tasks

Age	Developmental task	Challenging behaviors
	Being & exploring	
0 to 18 months	Grow and trust Explore their world	Cries Grabs everything
	Thinking & feeling	
18 to 36 months	Begin to separate Learn to express feelings constructively	Says, "No" Runs away Throws a tantrum
	Power & identity	
3 to 6 years	Decide how to be powerful Decide what men and women do	Refuses to cooperate Sets up conflicts and watches how people handle them Tries on different roles
	Structures & peers	
6 to 12 years	Develop a position (structure) for living in the outside world. This includes moral development with peers.	Challenges parents' values Compares, disagrees with, tests, and experiences the consequences of breaking rules

Four-year-olds have power struggles. These behaviors are typical for the age even though they are frustrating to live with.

With effective parenting the developmental stage will pass. Without effective parenting, the behavior may develop into a habit or a serious problem. See chart above.

Michelle's bossiness is common in 4-year-olds but not for a 10-year-old.

Kirk's anger is appropriate for a 2-year-old but not for an 8-year-old.

Willie's distress is common for babies but not for 4-year-olds.

Asha's behavior is typical for toddlers but not for 6-year-olds.

3. Is the behavior getting better? Here you need an objective measure. Count the actual frequency of the behavior, and notice context. Write your notes on a calendar or in a notebook.

Does Kirk hit once a day, twice an hour, five times a week? Does he hit friends as well as siblings?

How many times does Willie cry when Mom leaves him? Does he cry when Mom leaves him playing with Dad?

Does he hit when he's rested as well as when he's tired?

Parents' impressions are often colored as much by the parents' energies, upbringing, and emotional stages as by their children's actual activities.

If your child's behavior or temperament has changed significantly, it may be helpful to think back. How long has the new behavior been going on? What was going on when the behavior began?

Willie's mom thought back and realized that Willie's behavior started a couple of weeks after her mother died. His behavior might reflect his fear of losing his mother, too.

4. Have you carried out a well thought-out plan for dealing with the challenging behavior? Some parents expect, or at least hope, that children will outgrow difficult developmental behavior without any effort on their part. This rarely happens.

Your plan needs to include what you want your child to do instead of the undesirable behavior. Plan how you will acknowledge improvement, as well as set a limit on the behavior. You can use the problem-solving worksheet from this book to make a plan.

Kirk's parents might ask, "Did we develop a plan to teach him how to deal with his feelings appropriately?" (Note, the plan needs to be more than giving Kirk a consequence when he yells or hits.)

Michelle's mom might ask herself, "Did we try a plan to

encourage her to think of other's needs or to teach her to be cooperatively powerful?"

5. Does your intuition or gut tell you everything is okay? Parents often have a sense that "something is not quite right" when a problem exists.

Kirk's dad might think, "I know a 2-and-a-half year old has temper tantrums and strikes out at people, but I really feel this is extreme."

Willie's mother might think, "I know kids often miss their mothers, but I don't think he should be so frantic at 3 years old."

If you suspect a problem

If you think you might have a problem, first check with your child's regular doctor to see if there are any organic problems. (For possible organic problems, see "Organic disorders" on page 81.) If your doctor can't help you, he might recommend someone who can.

Then, if you do not find an organic reason for the behavior, make an appointment with a counselor for a behavioral assessment. The counselor may tell you, "He is typical for his age. Keep up the good work and this will pass." Or she might say, "I think you have reason to be concerned."

If you think there is a problem, find a counselor or therapist you can work with. There are many good counselors; there are also many who are ineffective. An effective counselor is:

- Experienced with behavior similar to your child's
- Experienced working with children your child's age
- Able to develop a rapport with your child

You can find counselors through mental health groups, churches, medical centers, and in private practice. Keep hunting until you find one that you think will work for you and your child.

Being an effective parent depends less on your child's behavior and more on your willingness to deal with the situations that arise.

Non-developmental problems

Four problems that can cause challenging behavior are organic disorders, family system difficulties, personal stressors, and school stressors.

Organic disorders. Some children have behavioral problems because their bodies do not function well. Organic problems can be diagnosed by a medical doctor. These conditions can cause communication difficulties, irritability, headaches, aggressive behavior, distractibility, fatigue, inattention, stomach aches, intense activity, etc.

Family system difficulties. Sometimes children's behavioral problems at home and in school reflect problems within the family itself rather than with that child alone. This can be seen in the following example.

John was very aggressive at home and in school. A therapist found that John's behavior got worse when his parents fought. John was worried that they would get divorced. Unconsciously, he hoped if they worried about him, they wouldn't have time to fight with each other.

Personal stressors. Personal stresses in children's lives can cause behavioral problems. Parents may be aware of the stress but not realize the impact it has on the child. In other cases, the parent may be totally unaware of the underlying problem.

- peer troubles
- teasing
- poverty
- disfiguring accident
- sexual abuse
- physical abuse
- lack of adequate supervision
- daily schedule changes

Non-developmental problems (cont.)

School stressors. Behavioral problems at home can originate from troubles at school. The problems may result from the school environment in general or because the school is a poor match for the child. As with personal stressors, parents may be unaware of either the problem or the extent of it.

- different learning style
- too much homework
- academic pressures
- unclear expectations
- grade competitions
- presence of drugs
- public speaking
- difficult teachers
- cliques
- bullies
- ridicule
- boredom

Wise words to end with

Children need parents who see them as unique, capable, and loveable individuals. This is true whether the children have siblings or not. Much of the challenging behavior that children exhibit reflects their developmental stage, rather than the existence of a sibling.

Make time to know each child as an individual. Children want to be special more than they want to be equal. Special does not mean better or equal. Fortunately, you can have many special relationships in your life.

Look for the underlying developmental needs of challenging behavior. When you identify the need, find ways to teach children the skills they need to be successful with both their sibling and the world.

Take care of yourself. You will have both the perspective and energy to deal with sibling hassles when you are rested, fed, and have some fun in your life.

Seek professional help when you need it. Serious problems do not go away without help. If you are unsure, get a "check-up" to see that everything is all right.

Remember, you are a loveable, capable person even when your children quarrel. Your worth is determined by what you do, not by what someone else does. A STAR parent is a growing parent, not a perfect parent. This book offers you tools to become a STAR parent.

Common questions (with answers)

The following are some of the common questions asked in my parenting classes or presentations.

Q. ***How can I tell the difference between the need for belonging and the need for power?*** *My four-year-old son, Adam, is very difficult at home, but at preschool he is a model child — gentle with others, assertive, responsive to adult directions, spontaneously helpful. At home he never listens. I have to battle with him to get him to do anything, especially when other people are around.*

A. Distinguishing between developmental tasks often takes a bit of detective work. Since Adam behaves well at school and not at home, he appears to know what is expected and can do it. So the question really is, what benefit does he get from being difficult at home?

My hunch is that he resists requests so he can interact with you. I think this because his behavior is more difficult when other people are around. If he complied with your requests immediately, you would probably turn to talk with someone else. When he resists, he has your complete attention as long as the conflict lasts.

You can collect more information by noticing what happens when you two are alone together. Does he continue to challenge you or does he cooperate more?

If he is pleasant when you are alone together, the developmental task is probably to belong. Your job then is teaching him the skills he needs to feel connected when other people are around. You could start by looking at how he copes when you leave him at preschool.

If his behavior is not cooperative when you are alone together, then the issue is probably power. You handle this by deciding what information or skills he needs to use his power appropriately. For ideas, see pages 67–71.

Q. ***I've heard experts say that rewards are bad, but you suggest using them. Is this really a good idea?***

A. Rewards are appropriate when used as part of a balanced parenting program such as STAR parenting described in the beginning of this book. However, many people overuse them or confuse them with bribes.

Bribes are given to stop bad behavior. Rewards are earned by appropriate behavior. For example, if a child is in the checkout line screaming for a candy bar and the parent gives him one to quiet him, the candy bar is a bribe. However, if the child wants a candy bar and receives it after waiting pleasantly until they are checked out, the candy bar is a reward. To get a bribe the child must scream first. To get a reward he must be pleasant.

Rewards, used in moderation, are an excellent guidance tool. However, they can be overused. Rewards are a bit like sweets — a little bit makes you feel good, but a steady diet is not healthy.

Q. ***Is there any harm in reflecting a child's feelings if I'm wrong sometimes?*** *What I mean is, suppose my child is upset that we are leaving a friend's house. I say, "You are disappointed it is time to go." However, he's really mad because I helped him put on his coat. Have I done any harm?*

A. Probably not. Children learn about feelings best by having them labeled in context. As long as you guess right much of the time he will understand your meaning.

Labeling feelings works like labeling colors — you make your best guess and move on. "You're disappointed that it's time to go" is like saying, "You're putting on your red jacket." Few parents worry about whether the jacket color is really red or burgundy.

You hope with time any errors you make will average out. However, if you have trouble identifying your own feelings, it may be difficult for you to help your child. You may want to find a friend or professional who can help you learn to identify and deal with your feelings. Then you can teach your son.

As children learn to identify their own feelings they will correct you if you are wrong. Once kids can identify feelings, it is helpful to focus on different ways to deal with those feelings.

Q. ***Sometimes all I do is enforce family rules and referee battles between the kids. Is there some way out of this?***

A. There are three common reasons why this may happen: unclear rules, inconsistent follow-through, and a child's desire to interact with the parent. We will look briefly at how to avoid each of these.

Clear rules. To be effective, rules must be clear and positive. Tell the child what to do, rather than what not to do. "No hitting your sister" becomes "Touch gently." "Don't grab your brother's toys" becomes "Ask to use William's books."

Predictable follow-through. When you make a rule, plan what you will do when the child breaks the rule. For example, "Touch gently or play alone." When you have a rule, you must follow through. Otherwise, children learn to disregard you.

Acknowledging appropriate behavior. Unfortunately, many parents expect good behavior, but they do not notice and acknowledge it. When good behavior is ignored, children may resort to misbehavior to engage their parents' attention.

For example, one mom had been telling her kids, "Be nice to each other," but the battles continued. When she began to look for appropriate behavior and praise it, things began to improve. One evening when she was putting her older son to bed, he said, "You really do want us to be kind, don't you?"

Q. ***How can I tell if my child has the people skills she [or he] needs?***

A. Look at the checklist on page 88. The more you answer "yes" to the questions on the checklist, the better your child's people skills are. When you have figured out what your child needs to learn, refer to the sections called "What children need to know . . ." (Chapters 4-7).

Q. ***Can I use STAR parenting with family hassles other than sibling issues?***

A. Yes, the STAR parenting process can be adapted to use with most "people" issues. You can read more about STAR parenting with young children in *Love & Limits* (see page 90). You may also receive a free "STAR Parenting" mini-poster by sending a #10 self-addressed, first class stamped envelope to Parenting Press, PO Box 75267, Seattle, WA 98125.

Checklist for sibling skills

1. Does your child know three constructive ways to get attention or to be included in activities?
2. Does your child have two people, other than you, that he or she can turn to for a sense of belonging?
3. Does your child know the difference between "tattling" and "telling?"
4. Does your child know nonviolent ways of establishing his or her boundaries?
5. Does your child know when to "defend" his or her boundaries and when to "ask for help?"
6. Does your child use a variety of words (more than mad, sad, scared, and happy) to describe his or her feelings?
7. Does your child have three constructive strategies for dealing with his or her strong feelings?
8. Can your child actively identify feelings in other people, using a variety of "feeling" words?
9. Does your child understand the difference between "personal" and "positional" power?
10. Can your child identify what kind of power (coercive, persuasive, or cooperative) a person is using?
11. Does your child know how to negotiate or solve problems in other constructive ways?
12. Does your child have three strategies for dealing with coercive and manipulative power?

Other interesting books

This list of books includes classics as well as newer material. Look for these titles at your library or bookstore.

Books on siblings

He Hit Me First: When Brothers and Sisters Fight by Louise Bates Ames. New York: Warner, 1989.

Loving Each One Best: A Caring and Practical Approach to Raising Siblings by Nancy Samalin. New York: Penguin, 1996.

Raising Brothers and Sisters Without Raising the Roof by Andrew and Caroline Calladine. Minneapolis: Winston Press, 1990.

The Sibling Bond by Stephen Banks and Michael Kahn. New York: Basic Books, 1982.

Siblings Without Rivalry by Adele Faber and Elaine Mazlish. New York: Avon, 1987.

Books on temperament and differences

The Difficult Child by Stanley Turecki. New York: Bantam,1985.

Living with the Active Alert Child: Ground-breaking Strategies for Parents by Linda S. Budd, Ph.D. Seattle: Parenting Press, 1993.

Know Your Child, by Stella Chess and Dr. Alexander Thomas. New York: Basic Books, 1987.

Normal Children Have Problems, Too by Stanley Turecki. New York: Bantam, 1995.

Raising Your Spirited Child by Mary Sheedy Kurcinka. New York: Harper Perennial, 1992.

Your Child Is a Person by Stella Chess, Dr. Alexander Thomas, and Herbert G. Birch. New York: Viking Penguin, 1965.

Guidance books

How to Talk So Kids Will Listen, & Listen So Kids Will Talk by Adele Faber and Elaine Mazlish. New York: Avon, 1987.

Kids Are Worth It: Giving Your Child the Gift of Inner Discipline by Barbara Coloroso. New York: William Morrow, 1994.

Love and Anger: The Parental Dilemma by Nancy Samalin. New York: Penguin, 1991.

Love & Limits: Guidance Tools for Creative Parenting by Elizabeth Crary. Seattle: Parenting Press,1995.

Positive Discipline A-Z: 1001 Solutions to Everyday Problems by Jane Nelsen, Lynn Lott, and H. Steven Glenn. Rocklin, California: Prima Publishing, 1993.

365 Wacky, Wonderful Ways to Get Your Chidren to Do What You Want by Elizabeth Crary. Seattle: Parenting Press, 1995.

Without Spanking or Spoiling: A Practical Approach to Toddler and Preschool Guidance by Elizabeth Crary. Seattle: Parenting Press, 1979. Second edition, 1993.

Teaching problem solving and negotiation

Children's Problem Solving Books: I Want It, I Can't Wait, I Want to Play, My Name Is Not Dummy, and *Mommy, Don't Go* by Elizabeth Crary. Seattle: Parenting Press, 1982-1986. Second editions, 1996.

Kids Can Cooperate: A Practical Guide to Teaching Problem Solving by Elizabeth Crary. Seattle: Parenting Press, 1985.

King of the Playground by Phyllis Reynolds Naylor. New York: Aladdin Books, 1994. (For children)

Raising a Thinking Child by Myrna Shure. New York: Henry Holt, 1994.

Telling Isn't Tattling by Kathryn M. Hammerseng. Seattle: Parenting Press, 1995. (For children)

Books for children about feelings and power

All My Feelings at Home: Ellie's Day by Susan Levine Friedman and Susan Conlin. Seattle: Parenting Press, 1989.

All My Feelings at Preschool: Nathan's Day by Susan Levine Friedman and Susan Conlin. Seattle: Parenting Press, 1991.

Dealing with Feelings Series: I'm Mad, I'm Frustrated, I'm Proud, I'm Scared, I'm Furious, and *I'm Excited* by Elizabeth Crary. Seattle: Parenting Press, 1992-1994.

Relax by Catherine O'Neill. New York: Child's Play Ltd., 1983.

Stick Up for Yourself! Every Kid's Guide to Personal Power and Positive Self-Esteem by Gershen Kaufman and Lev Raphael. Minneapolis: Free Spirit Press, 1990.

What Is a Feeling? by David Krueger, M.D. Seattle: Parenting Press, 1993.

General aids

Growing Up Again by Jean Illsley Clarke. New York: A Hazelden Book, HarperCollins, 1989.

101 Ways to Make Your Child Feel Special by Vicki Lansky. Chicago: Contemporary Books, 1991.

The Preschool Years by Ellen Galinsky. New York: Times Books, 1988.

Stress and the Healthy Family by Dolores Curran. San Francisco: HarperCollins, 1985.

Survival Tips for Working Moms: 297 Real Tips for Real Moms by Linda G. Pillsbury. Los Angeles: Perspective Publishing, 1994.

Traits of a Healthy Family by Dolores Curran. San Francisco: HarperCollins, 1983.

Index

More HELP!

Skill-building books for children and parents that promote peace in your family, from Parenting Press.

Children's Problem Solving Series, 2nd edition by Elizabeth Crary. Illustrated by Marina Megale. This series helps children learn problem-solving skills. Each book introduces a specific problem familiar to most children and then prompts the child to consider alternative solutions. ***I Want It, I Want to Play, My Name Is Not Dummy, I'm Lost, I Can't Wait,*** and ***Mommy, Don't Go.*** Useful with kids 3-8 years old. Each book is 32 pages, $6.95 paper, $16.95 library.

Dealing with Feelings Series by Elizabeth Crary. Illustrated by Jean Whitney. These books acknowledge specific feelings and offer children safe and creative ways to express these feelings. Each book features a choose-your-own-ending format, and shows kids what the outcome of their choices might be. ***I'm Furious, I'm Scared, I'm Excited, I'm Mad, I'm Frustrated,*** and ***I'm Proud.*** Useful with kids 3-9 years. Each book is 32 pages, $6.95 paper, $16.95 library.

Love & Limits: Guidance Tools for Creative Parenting by Elizabeth Crary introduces a simple problem-solving process known as STAR Parenting. Talks about kids' development and temperament traits, and offers practical guidance tools. Useful with kids birth to 8 years old. 48 pages, $6.95 paper, $16.95 library

More books and ordering information on next page.

More books on preceding page.

Pick Up Your Socks . . . and Other Skills Growing Children Need! by Elizabeth Crary. Illustrated by Pati Casebolt. This book shows parents how to teach responsibility. A job chart listing average ages kids do household chores helps reduce unrealistic expectations. Useful with kids 3-12 years old. 112 pages, $14.95 paper, $19.95 library

Kids Can Cooperate: A Practical Guide to Teaching Problem Solving by Elizabeth Crary describes how to give children the skills to solve conflicts themselves. Includes a step-by-step process to help school-aged kids negotiate. Dialogues show problem solving in action. Useful with kids 3-12 years old. 104 pages, $12.95 paper, $19.95 library

Grounded for Life?! Stop Blowing Your Fuse and Start Communicating with Your Teenager by Louise Felton Tracy, M.A. A mother of six and a long-time middle school counselor, Tracy shows parents how to communicate effectively with their children. Useful with kids 10-18 years old. *Parents' Choice* award winner. 164 pages, $12.95 paper, $19.95 library

Ask for these books at your favorite bookstore, or call toll free 1-800-992-6657. VISA and MasterCard accepted with phone orders. Complete book catalog available on request.

Parenting Press, Inc.
Dept. 610, P.O. Box 75267, Seattle, WA 98125
In Canada, call **Raincoast Books Distribution Co.,**
1-800-663-5714
Prices subject to change without notice.